Baby Shower

Celebrating the Birth

of

....

Due Date

. . . .

Names Ready For The Arrival

. . . .

Mummy's favourite food

. . . .

Mummy & Daddy

....

Grandparents *Grandparents*

....

Baby Shower Guests
&
Gifs

....

....

....

....

....

....

Baby Shower Guests
&
Gifs

....

....

....

....

....

....

Guests Comments & Words Of Advice

Guests Comments & Words Of Advice

Guests Comments & Words Of Advice

Guests Comments & Words Of Advice

Guests Comments & Words Of Advice

Guests Comments & Words Of Advice

Guests Comments & Words Of Advice

Guests Comments & Words Of Advice

Guests Comments & Words Of Advice

Guests Comments & Words Of Advice

Guests Comments & Words Of Advice

Guests Comments & Words Of Advice

Guests Comments & Words Of Advice

Guests Comments & Words Of Advice

Guests Comments & Words Of Advice

Guests Comments & Words Of Advice

Guests Comments & Words Of Advice

Guests Comments & Words Of Advice

Guests Comments & Words Of Advice

Guests Comments & Words Of Advice

Guests Comments & Words Of Advice

Guests Comments & Words Of Advice

Guests Comments & Words Of Advice

Guests Comments & Words Of Advice

Guests Comments & Words Of Advice

Guests Comments & Words Of Advice

Guests Comments & Words Of Advice

Guests Comments & Words Of Advice

Guests Comments & Words Of Advice

Guests Comments & Words Of Advice

Guests Comments & Words Of Advice

Guests Comments & Words Of Advice

Guests Comments & Words Of Advice

Guests Comments & Words Of Advice

Guests Comments & Words Of Advice

Guests Comments & Words Of Advice

Guests Comments & Words Of Advice

Guests Comments & Words Of Advice

Guests Comments & Words Of Advice

Guests Comments & Words Of Advice

Guests Comments & Words Of Advice

Guests Comments & Words Of Advice

Guests Comments & Words Of Advice

Guests Comments & Words Of Advice

Guests Comments & Words Of Advice

Guests Comments & Words Of Advice

Guests Comments & Words Of Advice

Guests Comments & Words Of Advice

Guests Comments & Words Of Advice

Guests Comments & Words Of Advice

Guests Comments & Words Of Advice

Guests Comments & Words Of Advice

Guests Comments & Words Of Advice

Guests Comments & Words Of Advice

Guests Comments & Words Of Advice

Guests Comments & Words Of Advice

Guests Comments & Words Of Advice

Guests Comments & Words Of Advice

Guests Comments & Words Of Advice

Guests Comments & Words Of Advice

Guests Comments & Words Of Advice

Guests Comments & Words Of Advice

Guests Comments & Words Of Advice

Guests Comments & Words Of Advice

Guests Comments & Words Of Advice

Guests Comments & Words Of Advice

Guests Comments & Words Of Advice

Guests Comments & Words Of Advice

Guests Comments & Words Of Advice

Guests Comments & Words Of Advice

Guests Comments & Words Of Advice

Guests Comments & Words Of Advice

Guests Comments & Words Of Advice

Guests Comments & Words Of Advice

Guests Comments & Words Of Advice

Guests Comments & Words Of Advice

Guests Comments & Words Of Advice

Guests Comments & Words Of Advice

Guests Comments & Words Of Advice

Guests Comments & Words Of Advice

Guests Comments & Words Of Advice

Guests Comments & Words Of Advice

Guests Comments & Words Of Advice

Guests Comments & Words Of Advice

Guests Comments & Words Of Advice

Guests Comments & Words Of Advice

Guests Comments & Words Of Advice

Guests Comments & Words Of Advice

Guests Comments & Words Of Advice

Guests Comments & Words Of Advice

Guests Comments & Words Of Advice

Guests Comments & Words Of Advice

CPSIA information can be obtained
at www.ICGtesting.com
Printed in the USA
LVHW050142020323
740758LV00004B/42

9 781912 641116